Fearsome
FISH

Fearsome
FISH

Written by Steve Parker

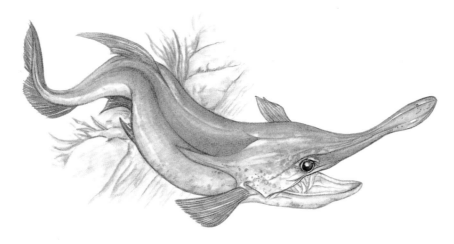

Scientific Consultant Joyce Pope
Illustrated by Ann Savage
and Chris Orr Illustration

RSVP

**RAINTREE
STECK-VAUGHN**
P U B L I S H E R S
The Steck-Vaughn Company

Austin, Texas

Library of Congress Cataloging-in-Publication Data
Parker, Steve.
Fearsome fish / written by Steve Parker; illustrated by Ann Savage.
p. cm. — (Creepy creatures)
Includes index.
Summary: Discusses sharks; the big ocean fish, including the whale shark;
game fish, such as the marlin; predators; rays; eels; anglerfish; and venomous fish.
ISBN 0-8114-2346-8
1. Fishes—Miscellanea—Juvenile literature. 2. Dangerous fishes—Miscellanea—Juvenile literature.
[1. Fishes. 2. Dangerous marine animals.]
I. Savage, Ann, 1951- ill. II. Title. III. Series: Parker, Steve. Creepy creatures.
QL617.2.P36   1994
597—dc20   93-28905   CIP   AC

Editors: Wendy Madgwick, Susan Wilson
Designer: Janie Louise Hunt

Color reproduction by Global Colour, Malaysia
Printed by L.E.G.O., Vicenza, Italy
Bound in the United States
1 2 3 4 5 6 7 8 9 0 LE 98 97 96 95 94

Contents

Fearsome Fish 6

Shark Attack! 8

Ocean Giants 10

Hooked! 12

Freshwater Monsters 14

All Mouth and Teeth 16

Rays Amaze 18

Fish Out of Water.. 20

Lazybones! 22

Venomous Fish 24

A Deal of Eels 26

Flashing Fins 28

Awesome Anglers 30

Denizens of the Deep....................................... 32

Glossary 34

Index 36

Fearsome Fish

Peer into a lake, river, or ocean. You may not be able to see much. But under the surface, there is a watery world of creatures living their fascinating lives. Like animals on land, they breathe, feed, hunt, escape, fight, court, and breed. The rulers of this underwater kingdom are the fish.

▶ What is a fish? This **Northern pike** has all the main fishy features. These are a backbone, fins and tail, and gills for breathing underwater. Like all fish it's cold-blooded. The pike grows to about 5 feet (1.5m) long.

The fins on the back are called dorsal fins. The **pike** has only one dorsal fin, set at the rear, near its tail.

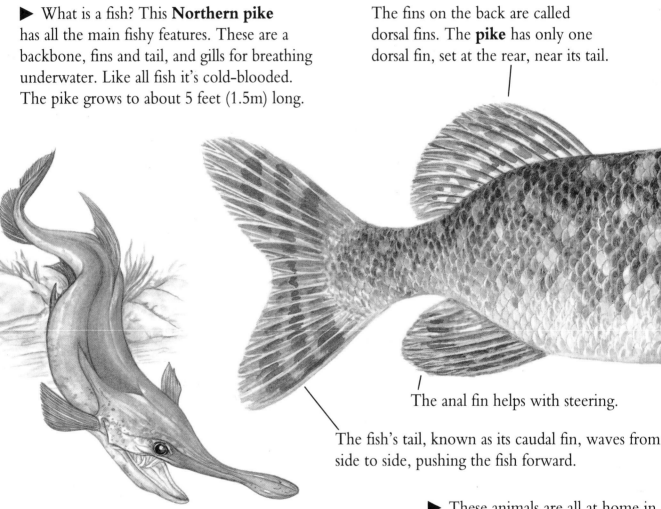

The anal fin helps with steering.

The fish's tail, known as its caudal fin, waves from side to side, pushing the fish forward.

▲ The **paddlefish** has an amazingly long nose, like a flat spoon. It opens its mouth wide and swallows any tiny creatures floating in the water. Paddlefish live in the rivers of the Mississippi region and reach about 6 feet (1.8m) in length.

▶ These animals are all at home in the water. They swim and dive well and they catch their food under the waves. But they breathe air through their lungs — they do not have gills. They are not fish.

▶ Very few freshwater fish could survive in the salty water of the ocean. Likewise, ocean fish would die in fresh water. This is the **cod**, a common fish from the North Atlantic Ocean.

Every fish has a backbone along the middle of its body. This bends from side to side as the fish swims.

Fish take in oxygen through their gills, which are covered by the gill flap.

The **pike** has a large mouth with sharp teeth. This shows it is a fearsome hunter.

A typical fish has two sets of fins on the lower side of its body. The front pair are called pectoral fins and the rear ones pelvic fins.

Common seal, a mammal

Emperor penguin, a bird

Bottle-nosed dolphin, a mammal

Shark Attack!

You are swimming at the beach on a warm summer day. Someone sees a triangular fin slicing through the water. He or she shouts a warning. Suddenly, there is panic. It could be the most fearsome of all the fish in the ocean. Get out of the water, now! SHARK!

▶ The truly terrifying **great white shark** is not the biggest shark. But it is the biggest meat-eating shark. It grows so big — 30 feet (almost 10m) or more — that it can attack and kill almost any animal in the ocean. A human is a mere snack!

◀ Why does the **hammerhead** have such a hammer-shaped head? This shape may help the shark find its prey. This shark's nostrils, as well as its eyes, are set wide apart. Blood floating through the water reaches one nostril first. The shark then swims to that side, and so finds its wounded victim.

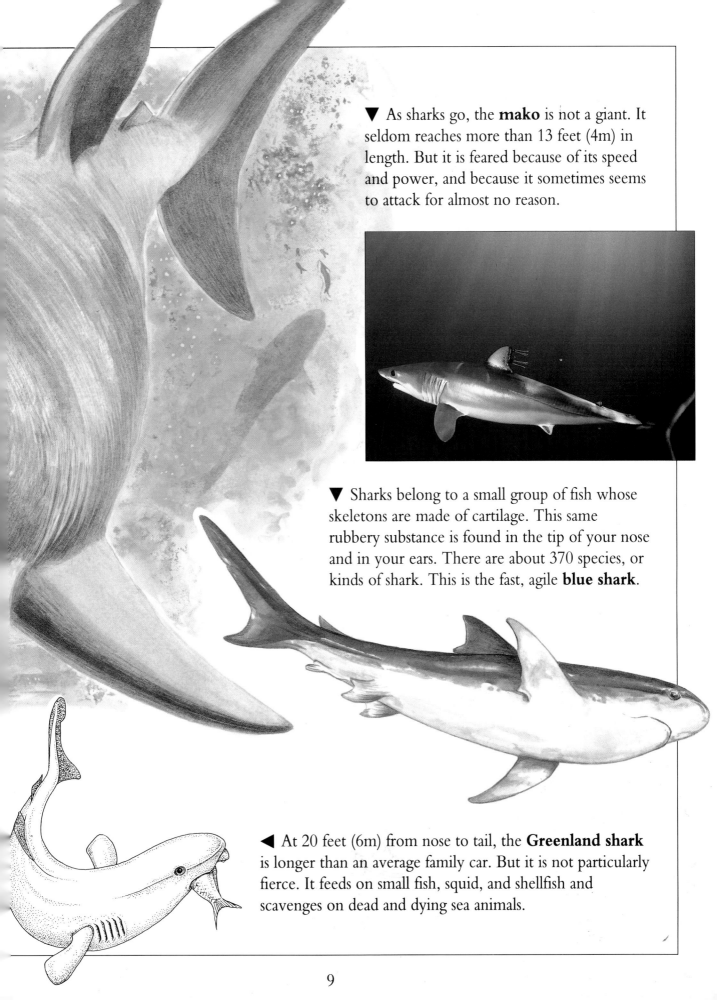

▼ As sharks go, the **mako** is not a giant. It seldom reaches more than 13 feet (4m) in length. But it is feared because of its speed and power, and because it sometimes seems to attack for almost no reason.

▼ Sharks belong to a small group of fish whose skeletons are made of cartilage. This same rubbery substance is found in the tip of your nose and in your ears. There are about 370 species, or kinds of shark. This is the fast, agile **blue shark**.

◄ At 20 feet (6m) from nose to tail, the **Greenland shark** is longer than an average family car. But it is not particularly fierce. It feeds on small fish, squid, and shellfish and scavenges on dead and dying sea animals.

Ocean Giants

Have you been lucky enough to see a really big fish? Then you may know how difficult it is to understand their size, as they swim in the murky depths. Here are some of the giants of the oceans. However, none is as big as the gentle giants of the deep, the great whales. But remember, whales are not fish, they are mammals.

▶ People eat herrings for food. But not a herring this big! The **wolf-herring** is as long as three 10-year-old children lying head-to-toe — and about the same width, too. It hunts smaller fish with its sharp fangs.

▼ The **basking shark** is the second-largest fish in the world. It can grow to 40 feet (almost 13m) long, and weigh more than 10 family cars put together. Like the huge whale shark, it feeds by filtering small living things from the water.

▲ Next time you see a school bus go by, imagine a fish about as long. At 50 feet (16m) or more the **whale shark** is the largest fish in the world. However scary it may look, it is quite harmless as it swims slowly along, its huge mouth open, feeding on tiny creatures. Sharks do not have a gill cover. They have a row of gill slits on each side of the head.

▶ The award for the roundest fish must go to the ocean **sunfish**. It lives in all the world's warm oceans and grows up to 12 feet (almost 4m) long, and 15 feet (almost 5m) tall! The sunfish eats jellyfish, shrimp, and small fish.

◀ The **giant beluga** are fish found in some Eastern European and Asian rivers and seas. In the past these fish could grow up to 24 feet (7m) long. But they no longer have a chance to grow so large. They are actively hunted for their flesh, and especially for their eggs. Others have been killed by pollution.

▶ The prize for the fish that looks most like a sea serpent would go to the amazing **oarfish**. A really long one is over 40 feet (almost 13m) from nose to tail. Its dorsal fin has a crest just behind the head. This fish swims by wriggling though the water like a snake.

Hooked!

Since prehistoric times, people have caught fish for food. In recent times, people have also fished for sport and pleasure. The sport fishers say that hooking a great game fish such as a marlin and battling with it for hours, is very thrilling. Other people disagree — they feel that these fish should be left free to roam the oceans.

▶ Imagine trying to haul in a rope attached to your family car. That is only a small part of the power needed to catch the spectacular **blue marlin**. At 16 feet (5m) long, it is one of the fastest and most powerful of all fish.

▶ The **black marlin** is even bigger and stronger than its blue cousin. One caught by rod and line weighed over 1,500 pounds (680kg)! All marlins have long, pointed noses called bills. The marlin may swish its bill from side to side to stun its prey of squid and small fish.

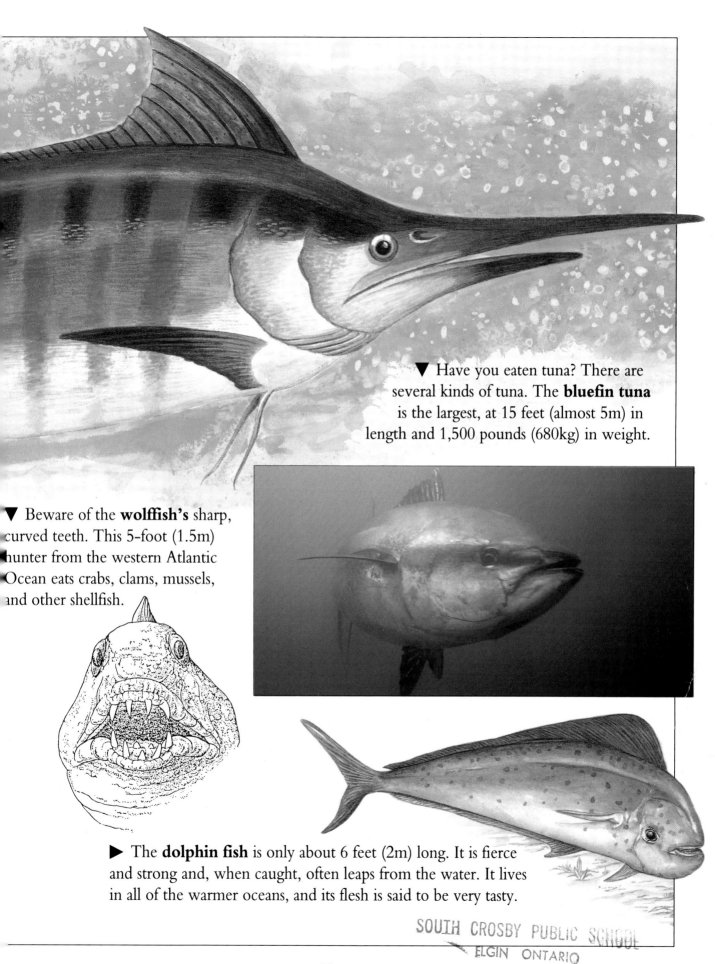

▼ Have you eaten tuna? There are several kinds of tuna. The **bluefin tuna** is the largest, at 15 feet (almost 5m) in length and 1,500 pounds (680kg) in weight.

▼ Beware of the **wolffish's** sharp, curved teeth. This 5-foot (1.5m) hunter from the western Atlantic Ocean eats crabs, clams, mussels, and other shellfish.

▶ The **dolphin fish** is only about 6 feet (2m) long. It is fierce and strong and, when caught, often leaps from the water. It lives in all of the warmer oceans, and its flesh is said to be very tasty.

Freshwater Monsters

The animals shown here are some of the largest freshwater fish in the world. They have inspired many fearsome tales in which they attack farm animals, pets, and people. But real attacks from these fish are extremely rare, especially nowadays. For these fish seldom reach great sizes today, due to pollution, overfishing, and many other hazards.

▲ The enormous **wels** or **European catfish** have a vast mouth and a smooth, scaleless body up to 10 feet (3m) long. The barbels, or feelers around the mouth, remind some people of a cat's whiskers and inspired the name catfish.

▶ The **Mekong catfish's** eyes are very low down behind its mouth. It looks as if its head is stuck on upside down! This huge beast is also known as the *pa beuk*. It grows to 8 feet (2.5m) long and lives in the big rivers and lakes of East and Southeast Asia.

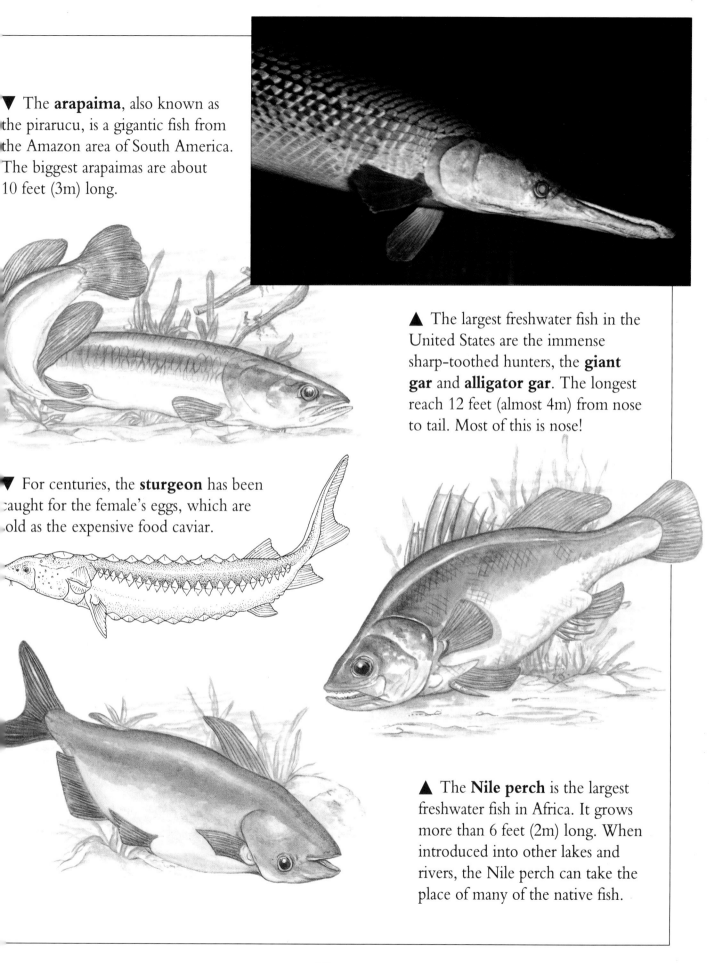

▼ The **arapaima**, also known as the pirarucu, is a gigantic fish from the Amazon area of South America. The biggest arapaimas are about 10 feet (3m) long.

▲ The largest freshwater fish in the United States are the immense sharp-toothed hunters, the **giant gar** and **alligator gar**. The longest reach 12 feet (almost 4m) from nose to tail. Most of this is nose!

▼ For centuries, the **sturgeon** has been caught for the female's eggs, which are sold as the expensive food caviar.

▲ The **Nile perch** is the largest freshwater fish in Africa. It grows more than 6 feet (2m) long. When introduced into other lakes and rivers, the Nile perch can take the place of many of the native fish.

All Mouth and Teeth

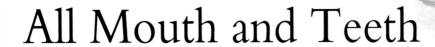

You can tell what an animal eats by looking at its teeth. Long, sharp teeth are generally the sign of a meat-eater. But if you got close enough to take a good look at the teeth of these fish, you would be in real danger! They are some of the fiercest of the fearsome fishes.

▶ Largest of the barracudas, the **great barracuda** has been known to attack people. A big barracuda is larger than an adult human. Its sharp teeth are ideal for grabbing smaller fish, as it hunts in the world's warm waters — especially the tropical Atlantic and Caribbean.

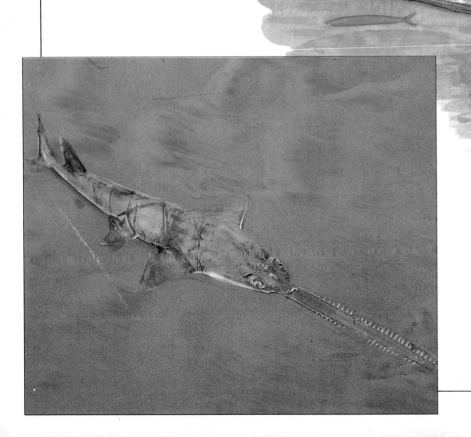

◀ The snout of the huge **sawfish** may be longer than you! It has about 50 sharp teeth around its edge. Some people say that this 20-foot (6m) fish slashes at smaller fish, to cut them up to eat. But most of the time, the sawfish digs in the mud with its snout, for worms and other bottom-dwelling animals.

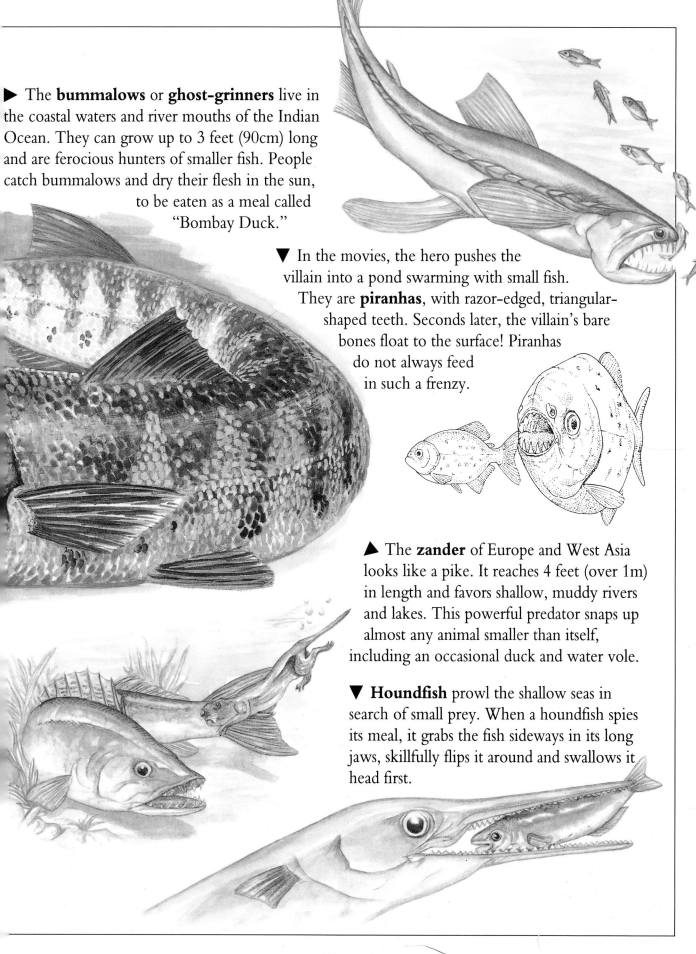

► The **bummalows** or **ghost-grinners** live in the coastal waters and river mouths of the Indian Ocean. They can grow up to 3 feet (90cm) long and are ferocious hunters of smaller fish. People catch bummalows and dry their flesh in the sun, to be eaten as a meal called "Bombay Duck."

▼ In the movies, the hero pushes the villain into a pond swarming with small fish. They are **piranhas**, with razor-edged, triangular-shaped teeth. Seconds later, the villain's bare bones float to the surface! Piranhas do not always feed in such a frenzy.

▲ The **zander** of Europe and West Asia looks like a pike. It reaches 4 feet (over 1m) in length and favors shallow, muddy rivers and lakes. This powerful predator snaps up almost any animal smaller than itself, including an occasional duck and water vole.

▼ **Houndfish** prowl the shallow seas in search of small prey. When a houndfish spies its meal, it grabs the fish sideways in its long jaws, skillfully flips it around and swallows it head first.

Rays Amaze

Rays are fish that look as if they have been squashed flat. They are low and wide, with flaps called "wings" at the sides of the body. But rays are not relations of the flatfish. Rays, along with sharks and skates belong to a primitive group of fish that have skeletons made of rubbery, gristly cartilage rather than bone.

▶ The **stingray** rests buried in the sand, then comes out to munch on crabs and other animals with its broad, crushing teeth. When alarmed, it lashes its long tail and jabs the saw-edged spine into the attacker. Poison flows from the spine, and soon the attacker is in great pain — or dead.

▼ The **electric ray** has special muscles in the sides of its body. They make jolts of electricity that spread through the water, stunning and killing small fish nearby. The electricity produced can give a person a strong shock!

▶ When a ray swims, it flaps its wings and seems to "fly" through the water. This is one of the most elegant ray swimmers, the **eagle ray** of the eastern Atlantic and Mediterranean.

▶ There are about 320 kinds of rays and their close cousins, skates. This is the biggest — the huge **manta ray** or "devilfish." It measures more than 20 feet (6m) across. The manta looks fearsome, but it feeds only on tiny floating plants and creatures.

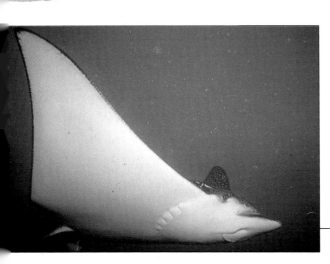

▼ Have you ever picked up a "mermaid's purse" on the beach? It is probably the egg case of a shark, ray, or skate. The mother skate lays the eggs so their tendrils tangle around rocks or weeds. The baby skates develop inside. They are about 8 inches (3cm) long when they hatch.

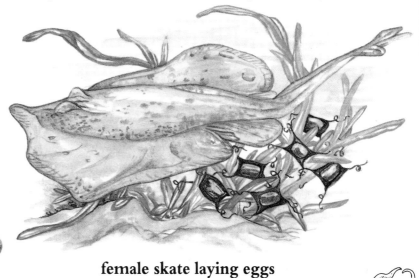

female skate laying eggs

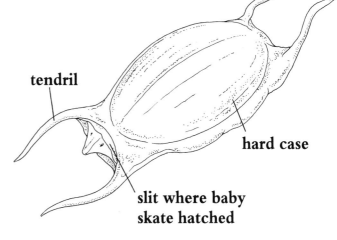

tendril

hard case

slit where baby
skate hatched

Fish Out of Water

Can a fish live out of water? Yes, if it is a lungfish. By gulping in air through their mouths these amazing fish can survive when their pools and ponds dry out. They take oxygen from the air into their bag-like lungs. When they are under water, they use their gills to remove oxygen from the water, just as other fish do.

▼ As its waters dry out, the **South American lungfish** digs into the moist mud. It makes a slimy bag around itself and rests until the rains and floods refill the rivers.

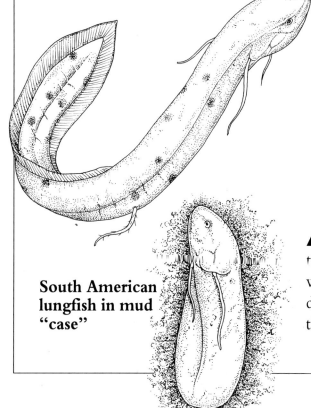

South American lungfish in mud "case"

▲ Like its South American cousin, the **African lungfish** takes gulps of air to get extra oxygen. It does this when its waters become too warm and shallow to hold enough dissolved oxygen. It can also "sleep" in the mud during times of drought.

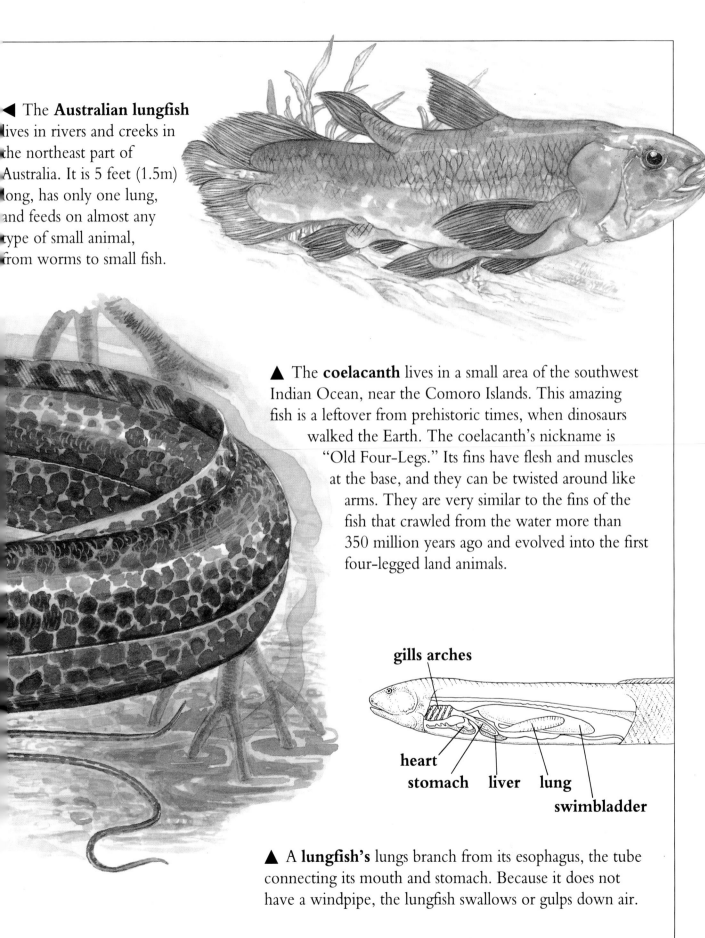

◀ The **Australian lungfish** lives in rivers and creeks in the northeast part of Australia. It is 5 feet (1.5m) long, has only one lung, and feeds on almost any type of small animal, from worms to small fish.

▲ The **coelacanth** lives in a small area of the southwest Indian Ocean, near the Comoro Islands. This amazing fish is a leftover from prehistoric times, when dinosaurs walked the Earth. The coelacanth's nickname is "Old Four-Legs." Its fins have flesh and muscles at the base, and they can be twisted around like arms. They are very similar to the fins of the fish that crawled from the water more than 350 million years ago and evolved into the first four-legged land animals.

gills arches

heart
stomach   liver   lung
swimbladder

▲ A **lungfish's** lungs branch from its esophagus, the tube connecting its mouth and stomach. Because it does not have a windpipe, the lungfish swallows or gulps down air.

Lazybones!

Being a fish can be a slow, lazy life. Some fish do almost nothing except lie around all day! They rest on the sea or lake bed, disguised as rock, weed, or sand. There they wait for their dinner to swim past, in the shape of a smaller fish or some other animal. With a sudden snap-and-gulp, the food is totally gone.

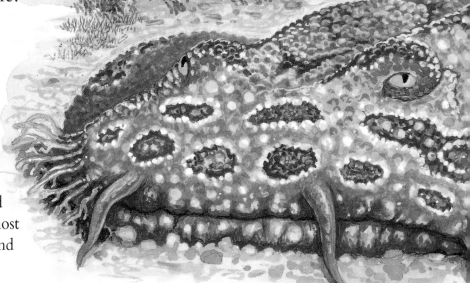

▼ If you lay on the seabed all day, you might think it would be sensible to have eyes on the top of your head. The **northern stargazer** has just this design. It can keep a look-out for small fish, crabs, and shrimp, even when it is almost completely buried in the sand or mud.

► A member of the strange flatfish group, the **dab** is quite small — only about a foot long. It feeds on worms and anything else small enough to fit into its tiny mouth.

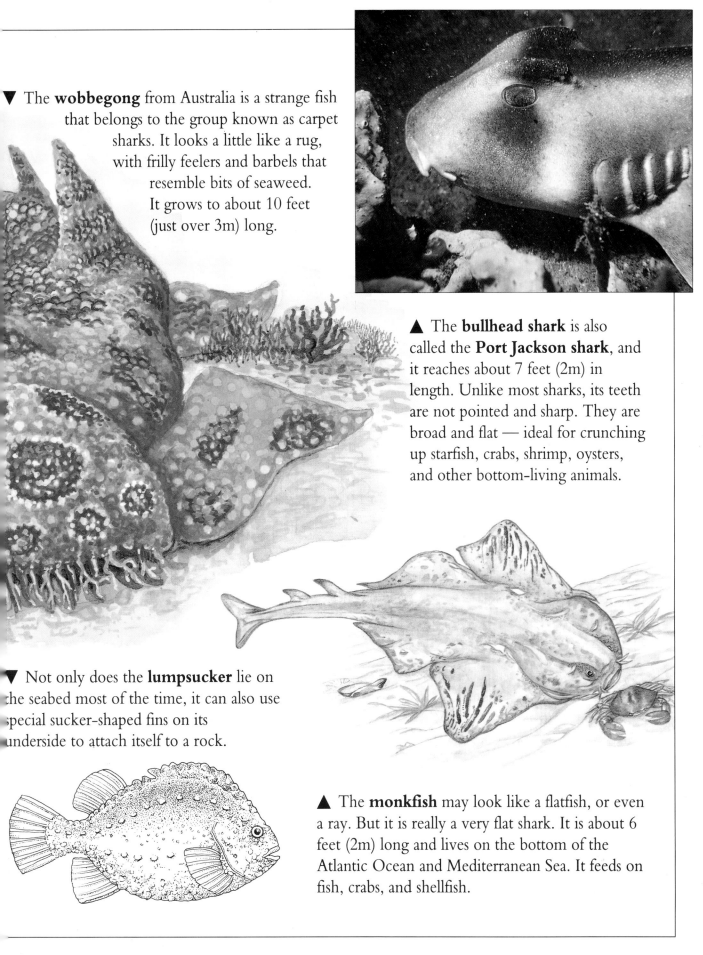

▼ The **wobbegong** from Australia is a strange fish that belongs to the group known as carpet sharks. It looks a little like a rug, with frilly feelers and barbels that resemble bits of seaweed. It grows to about 10 feet (just over 3m) long.

▲ The **bullhead shark** is also called the **Port Jackson shark**, and it reaches about 7 feet (2m) in length. Unlike most sharks, its teeth are not pointed and sharp. They are broad and flat — ideal for crunching up starfish, crabs, shrimp, oysters, and other bottom-living animals.

▼ Not only does the **lumpsucker** lie on the seabed most of the time, it can also use special sucker-shaped fins on its underside to attach itself to a rock.

▲ The **monkfish** may look like a flatfish, or even a ray. But it is really a very flat shark. It is about 6 feet (2m) long and lives on the bottom of the Atlantic Ocean and Mediterranean Sea. It feeds on fish, crabs, and shellfish.

Venomous Fish

Certain fish produce some of the strongest poisons in the entire animal world. Most poisonous fish live in the warm waters of coral reefs and tropical seas. Also, most use their poisons and venoms in self-defense, rather than to kill animals for food. The deadly spines of these fish are one good reason to wear sturdy beach shoes.

▼ The most poisonous fish in the world is the **stonefish**. It lies perfectly still, looking like a seaweed-covered rock, and waits for passing victims which it swallows in its huge mouth. The poison in its spines will kill any would-be predator.

▲ If you ever see a fish like this — stay far away! The bright colors warn you, and other animals, to steer clear. This is the **scorpionfish**, also called the **lionfish** or **firefish**. The poison in its fin spines can be deadly.

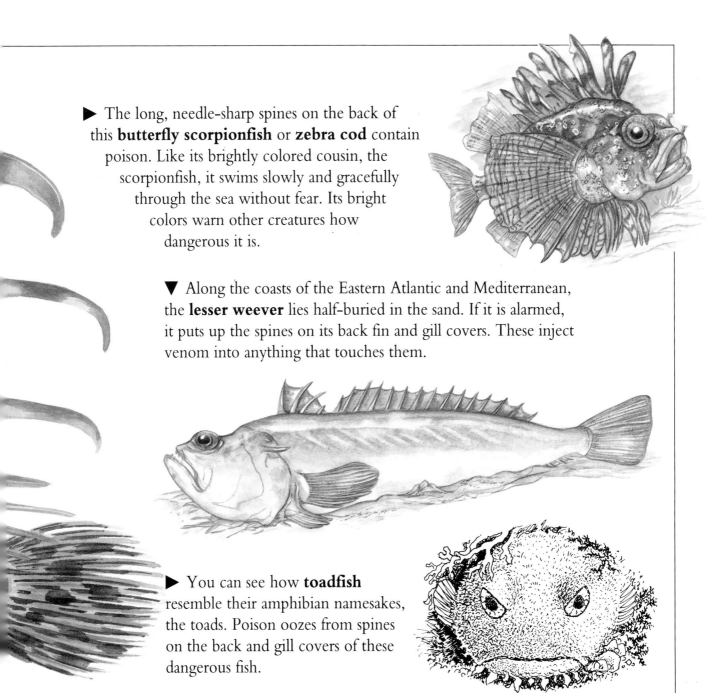

▶ The long, needle-sharp spines on the back of this **butterfly scorpionfish** or **zebra cod** contain poison. Like its brightly colored cousin, the scorpionfish, it swims slowly and gracefully through the sea without fear. Its bright colors warn other creatures how dangerous it is.

▼ Along the coasts of the Eastern Atlantic and Mediterranean, the **lesser weever** lies half-buried in the sand. If it is alarmed, it puts up the spines on its back fin and gill covers. These inject venom into anything that touches them.

▶ You can see how **toadfish** resemble their amphibian namesakes, the toads. Poison oozes from spines on the back and gill covers of these dangerous fish.

How did **pufferfish** get their name? When attacked, these little fish suck up water to become rounded, fish-faced balls. Parts of their flesh and inside organs contain deadly poisons. Predators — including people — who eat the wrong parts are in great danger.

A Deal of Eels

Eels are the snake-like fish found in both oceans and freshwater. They have long, twisted bodies with long, thin fins along the back and underside. Eels swim by swinging their slimy bodies from side to side. They can wriggle fast forward like this, and surprisingly fast backward, too!

▶ The **moray** can be fierce and fearsome, but only when it is prodded or provoked. For most of the time this muscular, strong eel, up to 5 feet (1.5m) long, hides in a rocky crack with just its head poking out.

▼ The **American eel** has an amazing life history. In fresh water, it grows big and wriggly on a menu of water insects, worms, shellfish, and small fish. Then it heads for the open ocean…

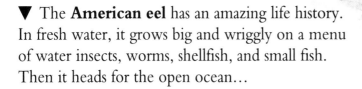

1. The full-grown eel swims downriver to the ocean, and out to the mid-Atlantic. It lays its eggs, and dies.

2. Baby eels hatch out in deep water as leaf-shaped, see-through larvae.

3. The larvae drift west for about a year to the coasts of America, growing and changing shape on the way.

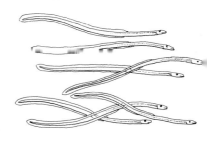

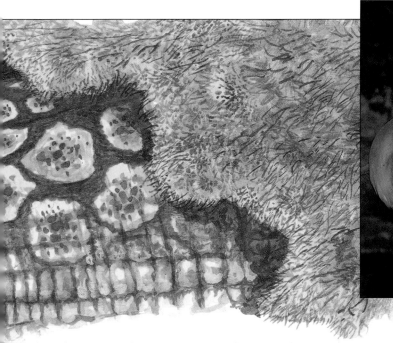

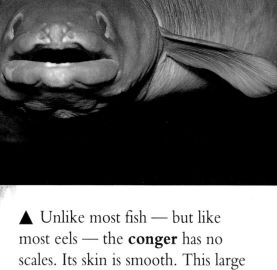

▼ The **electric eel** is not a true eel, it is a distant cousin of the carp. But it is electric! Special muscles along its body can make shocking 500-volt bolts of electricity to stun its prey. It lives in muddy pools and rivers of North America.

▲ Unlike most fish — but like most eels — the **conger** has no scales. Its skin is smooth. This large eel, up to 9 feet (almost 3m) in length, lurks in sunken shipwrecks and eats fish, crabs, and octopus.

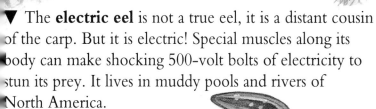

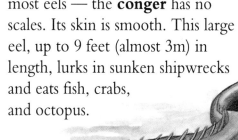

4. The larvae change into young eels, or elvers, and swim into the fresh waters of rivers and lakes.

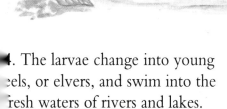

5. There, they grow into the adult.

▲ **Spiny eels** live in the deep waters of the Atlantic and other oceans. They are about 4 feet (1.2m) long and rarely seen, so not much is known about their life. Their main food is probably bottom-dwelling sea anemones, starfish, and worms.

Flashing Fins

How fast is a fish? For a few, the answer is very speedy indeed! Here are some of the world's fastest fish. They have slim, streamlined bodies and curving, crescent-shaped tails. Quickest is the sailfish, which can swim as fast as the cheetah can run.

▼ The **Atlantic salmon** can surge ahead at 25 miles (40km) per hour for a short distance. After living at sea for a few years, it swims back to the river where it was born to lay its eggs. On the way it may have to leap up waterfalls. Each leap may be as high as 10 feet (3m).

▲ The **flying fish** races along just under the surface of the water, to gain speed. Then it bursts out into the air, wiggles its tail furiously, and "flies" along on its large, outstretched fins. It can glide up to 300 feet (90m) before splashing back into the water. It does this mainly to avoid predators.

▶ You may think that this curious creature, the **sea horse**, is not designed for speed. You would be right! It is a real fish, but far from being the fastest, it is the slowest. Even if it waves its dorsal fin madly, it still only goes about 160 feet (50m) in an hour!

▲ When it shifts into top gear, the **sailfish** folds down its back fin. It can reach almost 70 miles (112km) per hour in short sprints. This fish grows to about 12 feet (4m) long and lives in all the world's warmer oceans.

It would be difficult to design a smoother, more streamlined shape than the **wahoo**. This warm-water speedster, up to 7 feet (2m) long, swims at over 45 miles (72km) per hour.

Awesome Anglers

Anglerfish angle, or fish, for other fish. The long, flexible spine on their head is a "fishing rod." The spine may have a lure on the end. Other animals come near to investigate the lure, and the anglerfish swallows them whole. The anglerfish group includes anglerfish, toadfish, and batfish.

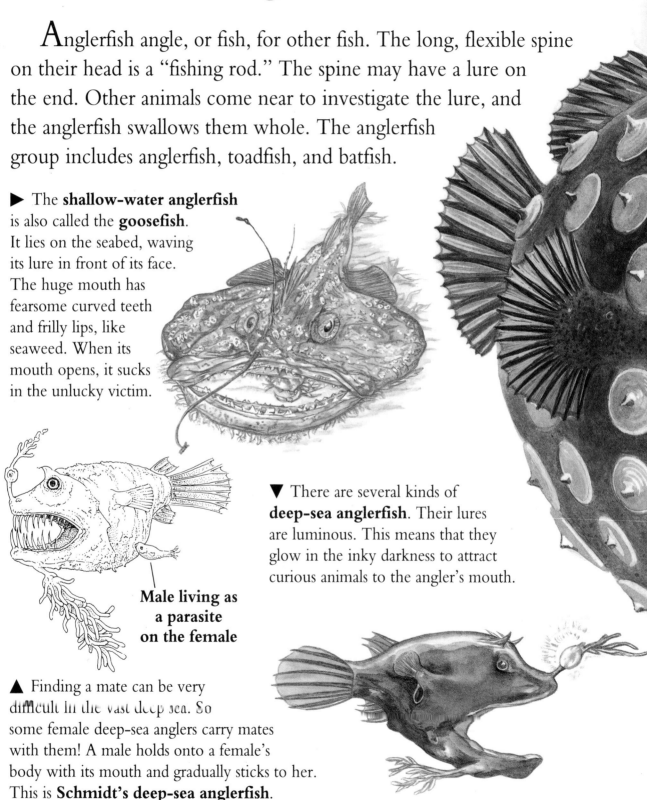

▶ The **shallow-water anglerfish** is also called the **goosefish**. It lies on the seabed, waving its lure in front of its face. The huge mouth has fearsome curved teeth and frilly lips, like seaweed. When its mouth opens, it sucks in the unlucky victim.

Male living as a parasite on the female

▼ There are several kinds of **deep-sea anglerfish**. Their lures are luminous. This means that they glow in the inky darkness to attract curious animals to the angler's mouth.

▲ Finding a mate can be very difficult in the vast deep sea. So some female deep-sea anglers carry mates with them! A male holds onto a female's body with its mouth and gradually sticks to her. This is **Schmidt's deep-sea anglerfish**.

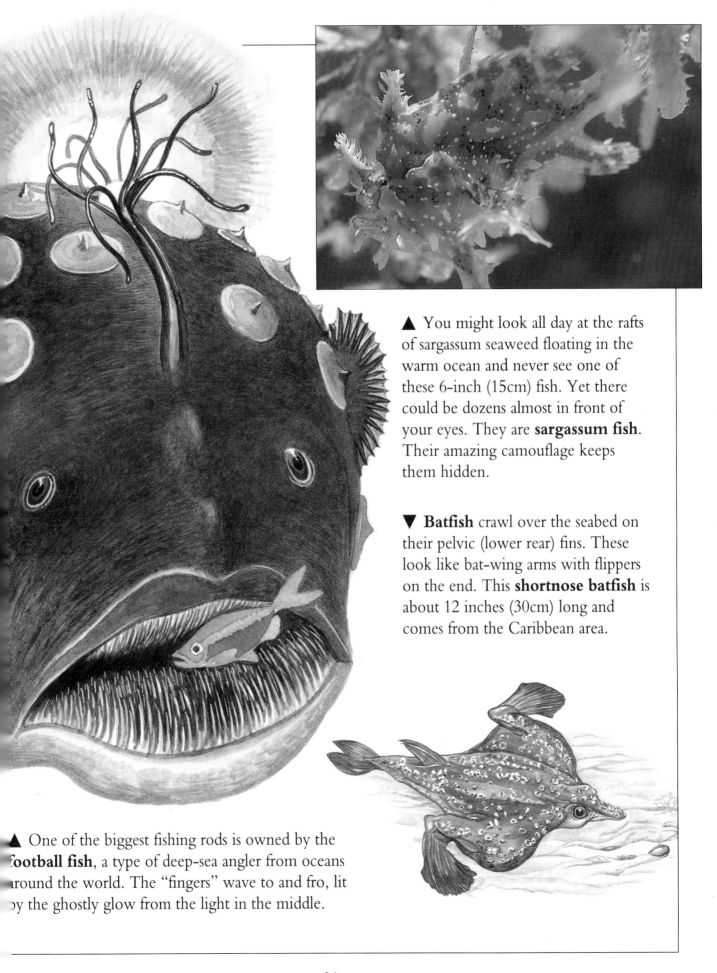

▲ You might look all day at the rafts of sargassum seaweed floating in the warm ocean and never see one of these 6-inch (15cm) fish. Yet there could be dozens almost in front of your eyes. They are **sargassum fish**. Their amazing camouflage keeps them hidden.

▼ **Batfish** crawl over the seabed on their pelvic (lower rear) fins. These look like bat-wing arms with flippers on the end. This **shortnose batfish** is about 12 inches (30cm) long and comes from the Caribbean area.

▲ One of the biggest fishing rods is owned by the **football fish**, a type of deep-sea angler from oceans around the world. The "fingers" wave to and fro, lit by the ghostly glow from the light in the middle.

Denizens of the Deep

In the dark depths of the oceans, many weird and wonderful fish hunt and hide from each other. Some of these fish are black and well-camouflaged in the darkness. Others have huge mouths and sharp teeth. It may be many days before they meet up with a meal, so they must grab it while they can.

▶ Almost all mouth and tail, the **gulper eel** is a good example of catching what you can, when you can. Its mouth is like elastic and stretches to capture prey much bigger than itself.

◀ **Sloane's viperfish** has fearsome fangs and a long scaly body, just like the viper snake it is named after. The long spine over its head has a tip that glows in the gloom, to attract prey toward its teeth.

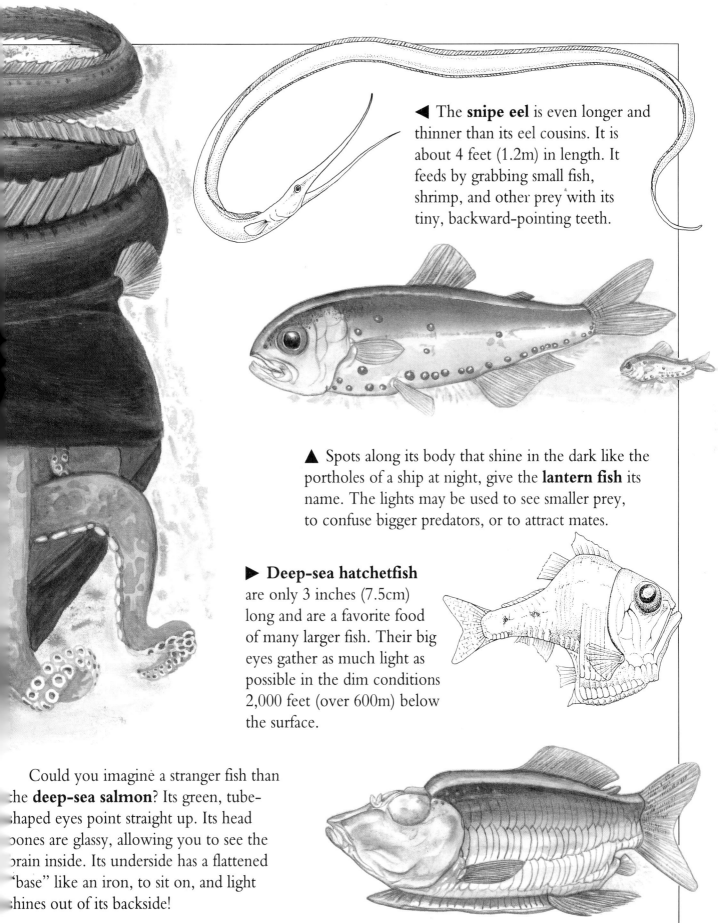

◄ The **snipe eel** is even longer and thinner than its eel cousins. It is about 4 feet (1.2m) in length. It feeds by grabbing small fish, shrimp, and other prey with its tiny, backward-pointing teeth.

▲ Spots along its body that shine in the dark like the portholes of a ship at night, give the **lantern fish** its name. The lights may be used to see smaller prey, to confuse bigger predators, or to attract mates.

▶ **Deep-sea hatchetfish** are only 3 inches (7.5cm) long and are a favorite food of many larger fish. Their big eyes gather as much light as possible in the dim conditions 2,000 feet (over 600m) below the surface.

Could you imagine a stranger fish than the **deep-sea salmon**? Its green, tube-shaped eyes point straight up. Its head bones are glassy, allowing you to see the brain inside. Its underside has a flattened "base" like an iron, to sit on, and light shines out of its backside!

Glossary

Anal fin The fin on the underside of a fish, near its tail.

Backbone The linked bones along the middle of the body of animals, such as fish, amphibians, reptiles, birds, and mammals. It can also be called the spine, spinal column, or vertebral column.

Bill In fish, another word for the long, pointed nose, or snout, of a fish such as a marlin or swordfish.

Camouflage Coloring or pattern that makes an animal blend in with its surroundings.

Cartilage A tough, rubbery substance that forms the skeleton of fish such as sharks and rays.

Caudal fin The tail, usually double-lobed, at the rear end of a fish.

Caviar Eggs of fish such as beluga and sturgeon, which are collected and sold as an expensive food.

Dorsal fin The fin on the upper side, or back, of a fish.

Eggs Small rounded objects that are laid by a female animal and that can hatch and grow into youngsters. Fish, birds, reptiles, and many insects lay eggs.

Fangs Extra-long, extra-sharp teeth, usually at the front of the mouth of animals such as cats, snakes, and fish like the viperfish.

Fin A broad, flat body part of fish and some other animals, used for swimming and moving in the water. In certain fish, these fins have become changed into spines, spikes, or long whips.

Flatfish Fish such as dab or flounder that look as though they have been squashed flat. In fact they are tall, thin fish that lie on their sides at the bottom of the ocean.

Gills Feathery body parts of fish and some other animals that live in water. Gills take in life-giving oxygen from the water, so that the animal can breathe under water. See Oxygen.

Gill flap or cover (operculum) A tough flap on the side of the head that covers the delicate, blood-filled gills on most fish.

Larva One of the stages in the life of certain animals. A larva hatches from the egg, is usually active, and eats a lot. In some fish, such as eels, the larvae look quite different from the adults.

Luminous Glowing in the dark.

Lungs Spongy parts inside the body of an animal. They suck in air when the animal breathes, and take the life-giving oxygen from it. Some fish, such as lungfish, have simple lungs.

Oxygen A colorless, invisible gas that makes up one-fifth of the air. Animals, including water-dwelling ones such as fish, need to breathe it to live.

Parasite An animal that feeds on, or lives off, another animal, and harms it in the process. The harmed animal is called the host.

Pectoral fin The fin on the side of a fish, near its front end, where its "arms" would be.

Pelvic fin The fin on the side of a fish, near its rear end, where its "legs" would be.

Predator An animal that hunts other creatures, called prey, for food.

Prey A creature that is hunted for food by other animals, called predators.

Scales The plate-like coverings in the skin of a fish, and on animals such as reptiles, and on a bird's legs. Scales are made of a horny material, light but hard, similar to your fingernails.

Venom Poison.

Index

A

African lungfish 20, 21
alligator gar 15
American eel 26, 27
    development of 26, 27
anglerfish 30–31
    lives of 30, 31
arapaima 15
Atlantic salmon 28
Australian lungfish 20, 21

B

basking shark 11
batfish 31
black marlin 12
blue marlin 12
bluefin shark 9
bluefin tuna 13
bottle-nosed dolphin 7
bullhead (Port Jackson) shark 23
bummalow (ghost-grinner) 17
butterfly scorpionfish (zebra cod) 25

C

carpet sharks 23
cartilage 9, 18
cod 7
coelacanth 21
common seal 7
conger eel 27

D

dab 22
deep-sea anglerfish 30
deep-sea hatchetfish 33
deep-sea salmon 33
dolphin fish 13

E

eagle ray 18, 19
eels 26–27
electric eel 27
electric ray 18
elvers 27
emperor penguin 7
European catfish 14

F

feeding 8–13, 16–17, 21, 23, 27, 30, 32, 33
fins 6, 7, 24, 25, 29
firefish 24
fishing 11, 12, 13, 14
flatfish 22
flying fish 28
football fish 30

G

ghost-grinner 17
giant beluga 11
giant gar 15
gill flap 7, 11, 25
gills 7, 11
goosefish 30
great barracuda 16
great white shark 8
Greenland shark 9
gulper eel 32

H

hammerhead 8
houndfish 17

L

lantern fish 33
larvae, of eels 26
lesser weever 25
lionfish 24
lumpsucker 23
lungfish 20–21
    lungs in, 21

M

mako shark 9
manta ray 19
Mekong catfish (*pa beuk*) 14
mermaid's purse
monkfish 23
moray eel 26
movement 6–7, 10, 26, 28, 29

N

Nile perch 15
Northern pike 6
    fins 6, 7
    gill flap 7
    gills 7
    teeth 7
northern stargazer 22

O

oarfish 11
ocean sunfish 11

P

pa beuk 14
paddlefish 6
piranhas 17
poison 24–25
pollution 11, 14
Port Jackson shark 23
pufferfish 25

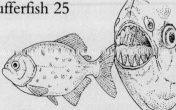

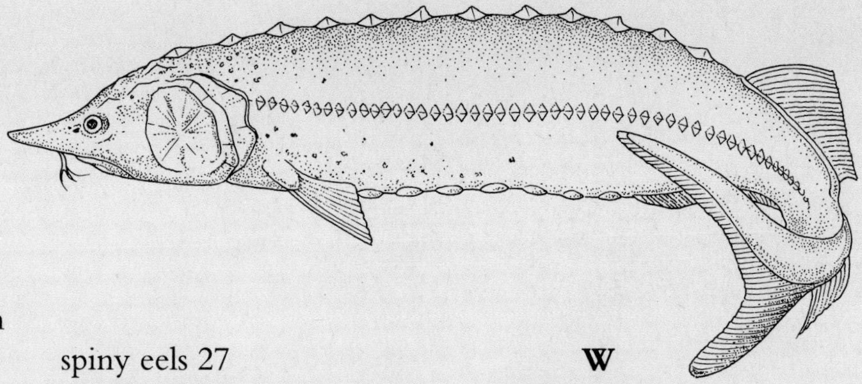

R

rays 18-19
    development of young 19

S

sailfish 29
sargassum fish 31
sawfish 16
Schmidt's deep-sea anglerfish
    30
scorpionfish (lionfish; firefish)
    24, 25
sea horse 29
shallow-water anglerfish
    (goose fish) 30
sharks 8-9, 23
shortnose batfish 31
skate 19
Sloane's viperfish 32
snipe eel 33
South American lungfish 20

spiny eels 27
stingray 18
stonefish 24
sturgeon 15
sunfish 11

T

toadfish 25

V

venom, see poison

W

wahoo 29
wels 14
whale shark 11
whales 10
wobbegong 23
wolffish 13
wolf-herring 10

Z

zander 17
zebra cod 25

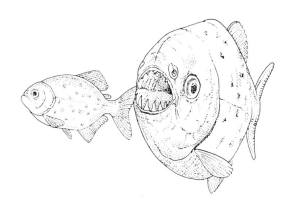

A TEMPLAR BOOK

Devised and produced by The Templar Company plc
Pippbrook Mill, London Road, Dorking,
Surrey RH4 1JE, Great Britain
Copyright © 1993 by The Templar Company plc

PHOTOGRAPHIC CREDITS
t = top, b = bottom, l = left, r = right
All photographs are from Frank Lane Picture Agency (FLPA)
page 8 I. Riepl/Silvestris/FLPA; *page 9* N. Wu/NHPA/FLPA;
page 11 N. Wu/NHPA/FLPA; *page 13* Planet Earth/FLPA;
page 15 D.P. Wilson/FLPA; *page 16* M. Ranjit/FLPA;
page 19t D. Johnson/FLPA; *page 19b* B. Wood/NHPA/FLPA;
page 22 D.P. Wilson/FLPA; *page 23* Planet Earth/FLPA;
page 24 FLPA; *page 25* Silvestris/FLPA; *page 27* D.P. Wilson/FLPA;
page 29 Heather Angel/FLPA; *page 31* Planet Earth/FLPA